Cryptocurrency

A Complete Guide To Making Money With
Cryptocurrency How To Make Money With
Cryptocurrency: A Complete Guide To Making Money
With Cryptocurrency

*(Learn The Foundations And Investment Strategies
Necessary To Succeed In The World Of Digital Currency)*

AngioloVisentin

TABLE OF CONTENT

What Are Some Examples Of Orphan Blocks?

One miner's discovery of another miner's VALID block at the same time might result in the creation of an orphan block. An orphan block is a VALID block. The system provides a sophisticated answer to this problem. Every miner is obligated to work on the section of the blockchain that is the longest, given that this is the portion of the chain that has received the most attention and effort thus far. If two miners discover a block at the same moment, then there will be two sections of a blockchain that are exactly the same length. Therefore, the miners divided themselves into two groups for a short period of time and mined on opposite ends. One group will almost certainly prevail if they are the ones to locate the next block first and then have the longest chain once more. The remaining block is then referred to as a "orphan block," and all of the miners switch to working on the chain that was just created. Such orphan blocks are not a significant reason for concern because the vast majority of transactions contained inside that block will also have been included in the other block; if they were not, however, they will be included in one of the subsequent confirmations nonetheless. Because of this, it is advised that one should not consider something to be genuinely confirmed until it has been blocked or confirmed many times.

WHAT EXACTLY DOES "MINING DIFFICULTY" MEAN?

Across the whole network of a cryptocurrency, millions of computers are working together to carry out a search that takes place several trillion times per second. When someone really does uncover the correct nonce, this is an instance of pure chance; nonetheless, it is possible to make mathematical predictions regarding when this will take place. For instance, the Bitcoin algorithm adjusts the mining difficulty (the complexity of the puzzle) every 2016 blocks to a time frame in which it takes the whole network around 10 minutes (= 600 seconds) to solve a block. This time window is determined by the number of blocks that have been mined since the last adjustment. The quantity of hashing power increases exponentially, which means that the difficulty of mining also increases exponentially. One of the defining characteristics that differentiates one cryptocurrency from another is the degree of difficulty of its mining process. Bitcoin achieves this goal by mandating that miners produce "blocks," which are essentially puzzles, in a particular format. To be more exact, they need to locate a nonce in order to ensure that the hash of the resultant block begins with a specified amount of zeros. The difficulty of mining increases proportionately with the number of zeros required. The complexity of the mining process may be altered in this manner.

The mining difficulty, in its most basic form, adapts itself to the hashrate of the network.

Negative aspects

1. The possibility of incurring significant losses One of the most significant aspects of day trading is the reality that novice traders frequently sustain monetary losses in the early stages of their trading careers, and many of them never advance to the point where they generate a profit. While the numerous investing and stockbroking platforms recommend that day traders only risk money that they can afford to lose, this recommendation is not universally accepted. In point of fact, many people who engage in day trading end up incurring enormous losses on funds that they borrowed, either through margined transactions or cash obtained from family or other sources. Their day trading business might suffer as a result

of these losses, which would also put them in a significant financial bind.

2. Substantial Beginning and Ongoing expenses: Day traders have to compete with high-frequency brokers, hedge funds, and other market professionals who invest millions of dollars to pick up trading points of interest. Day traders face enormous expenses both when they begin and as they progress. A day trader is left with few options under these circumstances other than to make significant investments in charting software, trading platforms, the most advanced models of personal computers, and so on. The fees for collecting live cost statements and commission costs that might accumulate owing to the number of trades are included in continuous costs.

3. Go into business for yourself: In order to make a living as a trader, one must first give up their regular day job and their reliable, regularly scheduled income. Working for oneself is the only way to succeed. After that point, the individual who invested their money in a speculative manner must rely solely on their knowledge and efforts to generate sufficient profit to pay off their debts and maintain a satisfactory standard of living for themselves.

4. High levels of pressure and the risk of burnout Day trading is a demanding endeavour because of the requirement to watch several screens in order to identify trading opportunities and then to react quickly in order to make the most of those opportunities. The requirement for such a high degree of attention and fixation can commonly

lead to burnout since it must be done every day without missing even a single day, and this must be done without fail.

The Evolution OfCryptocurrency

Bitcoin was the first decentralised digital asset ever created. Bitcoin is the most prominent name in the cryptocurrency industry, so it's likely that you've heard of it. Bitcoin, the world's first cryptocurrency, was created by an anonymous developer who went by the alias Satoshi Nakamoto. In 2008, Satoshi Nakamoto came up with the idea of Bitcoin and referred to it as a "purely peer-to-peer version" of digital currency.

Despite the fact that Bitcoin was the first cryptocurrency to be launched officially, there were other attempts to develop digital currencies years before Bitcoin was legally introduced.

Mining is the process through which Bitcoin and other cryptocurrencies are generated. Other cryptocurrencies may also be mined. In contrast to mine for ore, mining for bitcoins demands strong computers that can solve complicated problems.

Bitcoin was the sole digital money available before to 2011. Then, when Bitcoin aficionados started to become aware of the cryptocurrency's flaws, they came to the conclusion that they needed to create alternative coins, also known as altcoins, in order to enhance Bitcoin's design in a variety of areas, including speed, security, and privacy, amongst others. One of the earliest alternative cryptocurrencies, Litecoin aimed to be the silver to Bitcoin's gold when it was first released. At the time of this writing, however, there are over 1,600 different cryptocurrencies available, and it is anticipated that this number will continue to increase in the years to come.

Some of the Benefits of Using Cryptocurrency

Are you still not persuaded that cryptocurrencies, or any other form of decentralised money, are better to the traditional currency produced by governments throughout the world? The following is a list of potential solutions that cryptocurrencies, due to the fact that they are decentralised, may be able to provide:

Bringing down levels of corruption

When you have a position of authority, you take on a significant amount of responsibility. When you focus a lot of your attention and resources on one person or thing, the likelihood of that person or thing abusing the authority they have increases. According to Lord Acton, a 19th-century British statesman, "Power corrupts, and absolute power corrupts absolutely." Cryptocurrencies are an attempt to solve the problem of absolute power by distributing authority over a large number of people or, even better, across all of the people who participate in a network. After all, this is the fundamental principle upon which the blockchain technology is based.

putting an end to the excessive creation of money

When confronted with a serious economic issue, governments often have access to central banks, which provide them the ability to manufacture money. Quantitative easing is another name for this practise. A government that prints more money has the ability to either pay off its debt or cause the value of its currency to decline. The problem is that this approach is about as effective as putting a bandage on a broken limb. Rarely does it address the issue, and when it does, the potentially severe side effects might sometimes be worse than the problem itself.

When a nation, like Iran or Venezuela, creates an excessive amount of money, the value of its currency plummets, which causes inflation to skyrocket, and residents find themselves unable to buy necessary products and services as a result. Their money is equivalent in value to around one roll of toilet paper. In addition, there is a limited supply of coins available for use with the majority of cryptocurrencies. When all of those currencies are in circulation, there is no easy way for a central organisation or the company that is behind the blockchain to produce additional coins or add to its supply. This prevents either from happening.

Putting people in charge of their own financial decisions

When you use traditional currency, you are, in all intents and purposes, ceding entire control to centralised institutions and the government. If you identify your government as one of your assets, that is wonderful news; nevertheless, you should be aware that your government has the power to immediately freeze your bank account and deny you access to your cash at any moment. For instance, in the United States, if you pass away without leaving a legal will and you own a corporation, the government will receive all of your assets. This is the case even if you leave no other assets behind. It's also possible that some countries will stop printing banknotes altogether, like India did in 2016. As a direct consequence of this, when you use cryptocurrencies, you and only you will have access to your funds. (Except in the event that somebody takes them away from you.)

Eliminating the need for a middleman

When you send a typical money transfer, an intermediary, such as your bank or a digital payment company, will receive a portion of the funds. All participants in a cryptocurrency network's blockchain function as the transaction's intermediary. However, the cryptocurrencies' network members' pay is organised differently from that of fiat money intermediaries, and as a result, it is much lower.

Serving those who do not use banks

There are a great number of people in the globe who do not have any access to banking or who have very restricted access. The use of cryptocurrencies has the potential to address this issue by globalising digital commerce and making it possible for anybody with a mobile phone to conduct financial transactions. In addition, cell phones are far more readily available than banks. There are more people who possess smartphones than there are toilets, but the problem with toilets may not be solved by blockchain technology just yet.

knives and forks.

The event that takes place will be referred to as a fork, and it will relate to a blockchain. At a blockchain split, there are two different paths that are moving forward. Forks on the Bitcoin sorting out process occur predictably. Regarding the demarcation of territory What's more, the mining industry is undergoing upheaval. They occur at the same time for two miners working towards the same end objective at the same time. Similarly, an effect, the individuals momentarily branch in two different directions. This fork may make subsequently commanded to those modifications which typically selects the persons longest chain, consequently orphaning those additional obstructs included of the shorter chain (that were dropped eventually as a result of Tom's reading the individuals larger chain). A blockchain may potentially do the same thing to the worldview. At the developers, changing the underlying concepts that underlie the outcome used to determine which transactions are charitable.

Fork that poses a challenge.

In a similar manner A problematic fork will produce a modification for principles that enables producing new ends that are not identified as generous at the persons more prepared altering. This change will apply to each CoinDesk. When considering each individual Investopedia, An extreme fork statement refers to a circumstance that occurs on the other side of the point when a blockchain splits into two independent chains as a consequence of the utilisation of two exceptional sets for selects attempting to execute those schema.

Bitcoin XT (XT) in addition Bitcoin is a terrific both speculator and investor. An assembling in the square measure farthest point parameter known as a "hard fork" in the end Tom's researching Bitcoin focal point contributor Eric Lombrozo as a framework for get up and go scalability; nevertheless, support for both suggestions dropped around the same time. Bitcoin unlimited also suggests that there should be an adjustment made to the square degree restriction, which might lead to an untrustworthy fork being created.

It is possible for a stable fork to put together an arrangement even if the majority of the framework pieces do not follow those fork. On the other hand, Ethereum phenomenal collapsed due to a delayed result of a difficult fork on the Ethereum network. This fork could have been an effect of the hack on the DAO.

It's a delicate fork.

In the same way that a reliable fork is contradicted by a fragile fork, a fragile fork will make a modification respecting choices that will make bits noticed about outline meaningful to users who are using older software; in other words, it will be backwards-compatible. A delicate fork might be compared to some item that helps sort out individuals who disagree with the idea. When a non-upgraded item causes a block that is not recognised as significant in the end, Tom will examine the people's new fundamentals.

The scaling that was proposed takes place.

There have been several suggestions put forward for increasing bitcoin's achievement. Through the year 2015, Tom will undoubtedly be looking at the BIP 100. Garzik, Jeff In addition to this, BIP 101 Tom will eventually be looking through Gavin Andresen was presented to the audience. By the middle of the year 2015, a couple of designers were providing a bit degree most remote purpose with likewise optional similarly eight megabytes.

- Bitcoin XT could have been prescribed and secured about 2015; this should have increased the people' transaction get ready capacity for bitcoin; Tom's researching expanding those square compass cutoff.

- Bitcoin Fantastic may have been proposed for 2016 with Stretching those Transaction Get Ready Capacity Something LikeBitcoin at Extending the Individuals Square Degree Breaking Point.

- In 2016, a timetable that could perspective both the incitation of the disconnected Witness (SegWit) proposition made secured nearby december 2015 to Bitcoin focal point developers, and the headway of a square compass most distant perspective stretched if 2 mb, may have been produced by a simultaneousness to a part miners Furthermore developers conversationally termed "The hongkong Agreement." This timetable may have been produced by a simultaneousness to a part miners Furthermore developers. Nevertheless, neither of the deadlines was met.

• There are no limits on Bitcoin. Those that support the adaptability of the digger in order to supplement the bit degree breaking point Additionally has the potential to be realised through mining pools. AntPool, ViaBTC, and guru A. Ver Roger In addition, BitcoinUnlimited's supervisor and analyst, Rizun, reduced their pay. The Bitcoin infinite proposal will have a chance to be fascinating if it is coupled with the Bitcoin advantage in the sense that the individual bit size parameter may become not hard-coded, and instep the individuals' hubs. In addition, miners will signal for assistance from the compass that they are looking for by employing a thinking that revolves around a 'emergent concurrence.'Those who are in favour of the Bitcoin unlimited proposal argue that beginning with an ideology boundary limit purpose of viewpoint, miners need to further bolstering determine seeing the persons scaling result because they can be the folks ones whose fittings protect the individuals framework.

• BIP148 could have been a proposal that was mentioned or alluded to before. It could have been essential will create triggered around 1 outstanding 2017, and it gazed with drive miners for start disengaged Witness. an individual customer incited fragile fork (UASF) or a "populist uprising." It proved up to be unneeded in miners' perspectives, therefore they voted to incite SegWit utilising the people' BIP91 arrangement.

Is It Possible To Generate An Infinite Supply Of Bitcoins?

In a sense that runs counter to expectations, absolutely! But also, not at all. According to the regulations that govern how a Bitcoin transaction is processed, there are a maximum of around 21 million Bitcoins that may be mined. These coins are suitable for further division. The name "Satoshi" is given to the lowest fraction of a bitcoin, which is equal to one hundred millionth of a bitcoin. This fraction is named after the person who invented Bitcoin.

Where does it get its foundation?

In the past, gold, silver, or some other precious metal served as the basis for the currency most often used. If you gave them a $1, they were legally required to give you back an amount of gold equal to the value of that dollar. This was only true in theory. On the other hand, Bitcoin is not based on gold; rather, it is built on a series of mathematical formulae. People from all around the world are using various software programmes to generate Bitcoins by adhering to a specific mathematical equation. This process is called mining.

Anyone may examine this formula online, and there is no charge to do so. It is also readily available. Because this software has an open source, it will be possible for anybody to examine it and verify that it is operating in accordance with the specifications that were written into its source code.

Bitcoin: its Properties and Qualities

Let's take a look at some of the characteristics of a Bitcoin that make it unique from other currencies like dollars and euros.

Bitcoin is not controlled by any central authority. This indicates that it is not under the supervision of any one specific authority. Every device that is capable of mining Bitcoin and processing these transactions would join this network and become a node inside it. Each of the machines will cooperate with one another. This suggests, at least in theory, that no one government have the ability to seize the Bitcoins belonging to individual users.

Even in the event that a portion of the network is rendered inoperable for one reason or another, the flow of money will not be disrupted. The process of creating a bank account at any of the mainstream financial institutions often involves a number of steps. Another time-consuming and laborious step in the process is setting up the merchant accounts. When it comes to Bitcoin, you are able to generate a Bitcoin address for yourself in a matter of minutes and without having to pay any fees. In addition to that, it is rather anonymous.

Users are permitted to have an unlimited number of Bitcoin addresses, and these addresses are not associated with any users' names, addresses, or any other personally identifiable information. The operation of bitcoins may be understood without any kind of obscurity. The term "blockchain" refers to the distributed digital ledger that records every transaction that takes place on the network. This ledger is stored in the network. The blockchain explains everything. If your Bitcoin address is public, then anybody will be able to see how many bitcoins are kept at that address. If your address is private, then only you will be able to see how many bitcoins are stored there.

On the other hand, they wouldn't be able to tell who the address belonged to. On the Bitcoin network, there are several various precautions that you may take to increase the level of security afforded to your actions. Any overseas transaction with a bank would result in the charging of a transaction fee by the bank. However, this is not the case with the bitcoin. You will also be able to send money to any location in the world, and the recipient will have it in their possession within a matter of minutes.

The transactions on the Bitcoin network are processed quite rapidly. If you send Bitcoin from your account to another address, there is no way for you to receive them back once they have been sent. You will be able to acquire them if the recipient sends them back to you. If not, they will not be found again in any form.

It would appear that Bitcoin has a lot going for it, wouldn't you agree with that assessment? But how does it actually operate when put into practise? In the next sections, you will get further knowledge on Bitcoins.

Acquiring Knowledge of Ether (ETH)

Blockchain development is utilised by Ethereum technology, which is utilised by third-party internet corporations, in order to alter the storage of customer data such as bank information. A blockchain is a special kind of database that keeps data in chronologically ordered blocks. It was first designed to record transactions involving bitcoin, but now it is utilised as the foundation for the majority of the most important cryptocurrencies.

The goal of the Ethereum model is to provide users with an environment that is safer and more secure by preventing hackers from accessing the users' personal data. Ether is a means of trade, much like other cryptocurrencies, but what sets it apart from other cryptocurrencies is its capacity to be utilised on the Ethereum network to facilitate the computation of decentralised applications (dApps). In contrast to the possibility of exchanging other cryptocurrencies for Ether tokens, it is not possible to trade Ether for any of the other digital currencies in order to supply the necessary computational power for Ethereum transactions.

Ethereum facilitates the development of what are known as dapps, which are decentralised digital programmes, as well as their operation. To pay for the computing resources that are required to carry out these actions, you have the option of using ether tokens as payment.

Ether functions as a medium that enables payments to be made by a developer who is developing Ethereum apps and who has to pay in order for those programmes to be hosted and executed on the Ethereum network, as well as by a user who is utilising the application and who also needs to pay in order to use it.

The amount of network resources that were utilised in the production of an application determines the quantity of Ether tokens that a developer is required to pay. This is comparable to the way that an inefficient engine needs more gasoline, but an efficient engine utilises less fuel overall. Applications that use large amounts of data require more Ether in order to perform transactions. The amount of computing power and time that an application need to execute the activity is one of the factors that determines the Ether cost that must be paid. For example, the more computational power and time that an application requires, the higher the

Ether fee will be. The fee that must be paid in order for the transaction to be finalised is rather expensive.

The underlying ideals and applications of investing in Bitcoin are not always aligned with one another. Because of Bitcoin's steadily increasing value and the expansion of the market for exchanging it, many people have begun to view it as an investment, much to the way that some individuals invest in stocks. The phrase "investing in Bitcoin" is still often used, despite the numerous explanations and forums on the subject. The market has given rise to a great number of exchange platforms and even broker agencies, all of which will be discussed in the next chapter in their respective contexts. For the time being, we will concentrate on discussing what investing in Bitcoin looks like, why people engage in such behaviour, and what the implications of such behaviour are.

Investing in foreign currencies is not a novel concept. Gold, diamonds, oil, and the value placed on the US dollar are all examples of ways in which values may be represented yet can change over time. There is a demand for dollars from nations that do not utilise the US dollar as their primary currency. In these nations, the US dollar acts as an asset that individuals save up for and sell when it appreciates in value in comparison to the country's primary medium of exchange. In this respect, Bitcoin is the global currency that increases unlike any other, and individuals with just one Bitcoin might quadruple their earnings if the price continues to grow.

People have been attempting to mine Bitcoin and keep it as an asset in the expectation that its value would rise over time, after which they will sell it. Then, the first bubble burst, which resulted in significant losses and disillusioned users who had been under the impression that BTC would be an endlessly expanding source of revenue. As time passed, the market experienced its most rapid expansion around the end of 2020 and the beginning of 2021. This was mostly caused by businesses beginning to invest in Bitcoin (BTC) themselves and developing platforms that accept it as a payment method. Those who had one bitcoin in 2015 and held onto it through the bursting of the cryptocurrency boom in 2017 have now amassed tremendous quantities of the cryptocurrency.

Anyone has the ability to invest in Bitcoin, with or without the assistance of a broker. There aren't many parallels to be drawn with Wall Street here. However, before opting to cease investing in real estate and instead put all of one's money into cryptocurrencies, there are a few things that need to be taken into consideration.

The first thing that consumers need to take into consideration is the market's actual level of volatility. No matter how stable it appears to be, there was once a slip, and there is a chance that it may happen again. It calls for constant monitoring, sometimes even on an hourly basis. When prices soar to unprecedented heights, it reveals more about Bitcoin's dependence on external causes than it does about its potential to rise–and stay at a higher level–on its own.

Be careful to maintain the highest level of safety for your investment. Having offline wallets at your disposal is one method for accomplishing this goal. Even though Bitcoin's open-source nature makes it a relatively risk-free investment option, it is still a good idea to keep some of your coins in cold storage and utilise other precautionary measures.

Because Bitcoin is so widely used, it is important to familiarise oneself with the regulations and statutes that apply to the purchase and sale of bitcoin in their own country before engaging in any Bitcoin transactions. Before making any important choices, you should make sure you have done sufficient study on the laws and regulations that your nation has imposed regarding cryptocurrencies.

The use of bitcoins as a store of value does not appear to be going away anytime soon. If it continues to trend in this manner, then it's possible that only a small number of people will be interested in using it as cash for their day-to-day activities. There are a variety of potential outcomes and applications for Bitcoin in the foreseeable future. Time is the only factor that can reveal the final shape that this coin will take.

Wallets That Are Offline, Hard To Store, Or Both

Essentially, it's a USB stick that has your private key. Because it is offline and not vulnerable to hacking, it is seen as being extremely safe. The benefit of using outdated technology is that, since you are the only one with access to it, you may maintain confidential information.

However, there is a drawback as well. You won't be able to restore the data if the USB stick becomes lost or misplaced since it is offline. Likewise, if your gadget is reformatted, you can lose your money.

Paper Money

It is precisely what it sounds like—a paper wallet. Essentially, a piece of paper has your private key. It's offline, just like the USB stick. So, you can prevent hackers from accessing your private data. However, in the same way as the USB stick, if this paper is lost, damaged, or thrown away, you will lose all of your important data.

Thus, how can you ensure the security of your private key?

Whichever approach you decide on, you need to always keep a backup copy of your important information. Additionally, you need to update your software to the most recent versions. Additionally, you need to employ as many security tiers as you can. Don't only depend on your password.

Naturally, make sure your password is difficult to guess when selecting one. The best combination to employ is capital and lowercase letters, digits, and special characters.

Which approach works best for you?

It is dependent upon your demands and the type of investor you are. You may store your digital currency at an exchange, for instance, if you prefer to trade over invest. Ultimately, the money is never truly there since it is constantly being traded.

You might wish to keep your cash in a wallet if you want to keep it for a longer period of time. In this manner, you may effortlessly relocate it anytime you'd want to and check on it sometimes. If you possess substantial quantities of money, it is advisable to exercise caution and keep your money in cold storage to safeguard it against cyberattacks. Just make sure your gadget is secured in a safe or other secure location.

Access to Information Regarding Transactions

On eBay and other online auction platforms, bots, scalpers, bad actors, and criminals, as well as second-party transactions, are rather frequent. NFT tickets provide a straightforward method for acquiring actionable business analytics about the manner in which and the locations at which your tickets are being sold and resold. You can determine the precise time that the transaction took place, the specific address of the digital wallets that were used, the amount that was exchanged, and a lot of other information as well. NFT transactions are not anonymous, despite the widespread belief that this is the case. There are a number of private companies, such as Chainalysis and CipherTrace, that provide blockchainbusiness intelligence solutions to its customers.

Costs of Tickets That Are Lower

Instead than being mined, NFTs are produced through minting. This is a technical difference that is not easily dismissed. Tickets for the New York Transit Authority (NFT) may now be printed for less than ten cents each, and the cost of producing NFT tickets will continue to fall.

Additional Financial Gains

Naturally, you are able to mint NFT tickets in order to use them as independent digital items. However, you can also utilize NFT tickets to provide fans access to an auction where they have the opportunity to bid on more NFTs that include more value exclusive material. Because NFTs are able to gather data from the first party, they may also be integrated into loyalty programs to provide additional benefits. There will be a need for some testing to be done on the marketing strategies, but the technology capacity is already there.

Opportunities in Marketing that are Driven by Data

Currently, if you buy six tickets to a sports event and bring five members of your family or friends with you, the ticket seller will have a commercial connection with you but will not have any information about the other five individuals in your group. That may be altered by the use of NFTs. If it was necessary for each attendee to submit an NFT in order to get entry, then each individual would need to move the NFT into their own personal digital wallet. The collection of a large quantity of actionable first-party data by NFTs is contingent on the manner in which the business logic was written as well as the specific data that was requested from customers as a prerequisite to the purchase of tickets.

Opportunities for Defi Deficit

NFTs may be purchased, sold, exchanged, swapped, used as collateral, borrowed, loaned, etc. in a variety of contexts. To put it another way, the only things that may restrict your capacity to use financial engineering to produce more value are the extent of your inventiveness and the degree to which your audience is prepared to engage. The capacity of the blockchain to democratize financial systems is one of the aspects that contribute to the technology's status as being great, super-exciting, super-dangerous, and super-volatile. It is also the reason why governments and regulatory agencies all around the globe are paying attention to the world of cryptocurrencies and DeFi (decentralized finance), in general.

The Next Step in Marketing

Next-level marketers will have the chance to let their imaginations run wild, regardless of whether their target audience is a community of interest, a community of practice, or a community of passion. What is it that your audience places the greatest importance on? How can you make them feel more empowered to participate? What further benefits can you make available to them via your assistance? Which kind of customer loyalty program represents the future generation? How much "access" to the main attraction will they be able to obtain? Smart contracts will provide innovative marketers with the tools they need to develop new sorts of marketing programs that are designed with components that are continuously automated and contribute to value generation.

The Prospects For The Long-Term Use Of Digital Currencies

The distributed and decentralized nature of a cryptocurrency's network is perhaps the most important aspect to take into consideration while learning about cryptocurrencies. With the expansion of the internet, we may be just'seeing the 'tip of the iceberg' in respect to future innovation, which may leverage the potential for permitting decentralization but at a hitherto unknown or unthinkable scale. This might be a result of the fact that we are just'seeing the 'tip of the iceberg' in regard to future innovation. Therefore, although in the past there was a need for a vast network, it was only achievable by using a hierarchical structure. As a consequence, there was a need of 'urrendering the power' of that network to a small number of people who had a controlling interest. However, this is no longer necessary. One may argue that Bitcoin symbolizes the decentralization of monetary systems as well as the shift toward more straightforward organizational structures. Bitcoin is an important technological innovation on par with peer-to-peer file sharing and internet telephony (like Skype, for example).

There is very little explicitly produced legal regulation for digital or virtual currency; however, there is a wide range of existing laws that may apply depending on the legal financial framework of the country. These laws include taxation, banking and money-transmitting regulation, securities regulation, criminal and/or civil law, consumer rights and protection, prison regulation, commodity and stock regulation, and other laws. Therefore, the two most important questions concerning bitcoin are whether or not it can be regarded as a form of legal tender, and whether it can be classified as an asset, whether or not it can be classified as property. It is common practice for nations to explicitly define money as the legal tender of another nation (for example, the US dollar), which prevents such nations from recognizing other 'currencies' as technically a currency. Germany is a notable exception to this rule since it allows for the idea of a 'unit of account,' which may therefore be used as a kind of 'private money,' and it can be used in'multilateral clearing circle,' among other applications. To look at it from the opposite perspective, if it were to be considered property, the most obvious difference would be that, in contrast to property, digital currencies may be divided up into much smaller amounts. This is not the case with property. Digital currencies are often accepted in developed economies because of their open financial systems. The United States of America has been given the most advice and has a significant presence on the map below. Economies that are governed by capital are considered to be either contentious or hospitable by definition. The question has not yet been answered for several countries in Africa and a few other places across the world.

Beginning with the fundamentals of democratic participation, it is immediately obvious that bitcoin does not satisfy the positive social impact component of such a purpose. This is because bitcoin's value is not one it can exert influence on, but rather is subject to the forces of the market. Nevertheless, any "new" crypto-currency could be able to provide democratic participation if the virtual currency has different norms of administration and issuance based on democratic ideals that are more traditionally based in society.

So what if a "digital" currency could provide a valid alternative to existing forms of money in performing the role of contributing positively to: the goal of promoting a socially inclusive culture, the equanimity of opportunity, and the promotion of mutualism; all of which, as their very names imply, are alternatives and/or complementary to an official or national sovereign currency? Although they are still in their infancy, the rate of innovation in the field of cryptocurrencies has been dramatic. Virtual cryptocurrencies like as bitcoin represent a new and emerging dynamic in the system.

After a coin has been dropped, the moment to purchase it is at its lowest price.

Why? Because those individuals who didn't cash out during the pump (also known as "bag holders") don't want to sell their currency at the bottom, when it would fetch a far lower price. It should go without saying that if the price of a currency you've bought moves fast upward, the best thing to do is cash out and put the money back into bitcoin. And if it's a good coin and you want to invest in it for the long term, you should definitely consider buying more after a price drop. Because a good coin will always increase again, it is often better to concentrate on acquiring good coin rather than making more Bitcoin. This is because Bitcoin's value is volatile.

REMARKS IN CONCLUSION

The process through which Bitcoin came into being is a very fascinating one. In contrast to gold, which must be extracted from the ground via mining, cryptocurrency is nothing more than an entry in a digital ledger that is distributed among several computers all over the world. These entries have to be'mined' using a mathematical algorithm. Individual users or, more often, a group of users may undertake computer analysis in order to locate certain data blocks. These blocks are referred to as eries. The'miner' seeks for data in order to produce a certain pattern that corresponds to the cryptographic algorithm. After that, it was applied to the erie, and at that time, they discovered a roadblock. Unencrypting a block of data requires first finding an equivalent data erie on the block that matches up with the algorithm. The miner is rewarded with a certain quantity of the cryptocurrency they mined. As time passes, the total amount of the reward will decrease as the difficulty of mining the cryptocurrency increases. In addition to that, the level of difficulty of the algorithm used in the process of searching for new blocks has been increased. From a computational standpoint, it is becoming more difficult to discover a matching erie. Both of these "scenarios" coming together will have the effect of slowing down the rate at which new cryptocurrency is produced. This replicates the difficulty and scarcity of extracting a resource such as gold from the ground.

Mining is now open to anybody and everyone. The person who created Bitcoin made the mining tool open source, which means that anybody may use it for free. Nevertheless, the computer that they utilize operates continuously, day and night, seven days a week. The algorithms are exceedingly complicated, and the central processing unit is working at maximum capacity. A significant number of users have specialized computers that were built for the sole purpose of mining cryptocurrency. The term "miner" refers to both the user and the specialized computer being used.

The human miner is responsible for maintaining a ledger of transactions and performing auditing duties to ensure that a currency is not replicated in any way. This prevents the system from being hacked and from behaving in an uncontrolled manner. They are compensated for their efforts by being given new bitcoin on a weekly basis, provided that they continue to maintain their operation. They save their cryptocurrency in a "pecialized file" on their own computer or any other devices that they use personally. The e-files are referred to as wallets.

Let's go over some of the definitions we've picked up, starting with the most important ones:

e-currency, also known as virtual currency or digital currency.

Fiat money is any kind of legal tender; it is backed by the government and is utilized in the banking system.

Bitcoin is the first cryptocurrency ever created and is the industry standard today.

Altcoin is short for "alternative coin," and refers to alternative cryptocurrencies that are modeled after Bitcoin's procedures but have subtle differences in their code.

- Miner: a person or group of individuals that mine digital currency using their own resources (computers, power, and/or pace). Miners may work alone or in groups.

- A wallet is a small file that resides on your computer and is used to hold digital currency.

In a nutshell, we may conceptualize the bitcoin system as follows:

- The use of digital currency.

- Obtained by the mining efforts of solitary individuals who make use of their own resources to locate the coins.

- A predetermined, limited system of currency. For instance, there can never be more than 21,000,000 Bitcoin generated in the whole world.

- Does not need the involvement of any government or bank in order to function properly.

- Pricing is determined by the total number of coins that have been discovered and used, which is then mixed with the amount of interest shown by the general public in purchasing them.

There are many other varieties of crypto currency, with Bitcoin being the earliest and most well-known of them.

- Can bring in a lot of money, but like any other investment, there is some risk involved.

The idea behind cryptocurrencies is one that a lot of people find to be fascinating. It's a fresh industry that many of them see as having the potential to become their next big moneymaker. You have come across the appropriate report if you believe that cryptocurrency is something that you would be interested in learning more about. Having said that, I feel like I've just scratched the surface with my article. What I've covered in this article is just the tip of the iceberg when it comes to cryptocurrency.

Your trusted ally is known as "Two-Factor Authentication." If you want to engage in any kind of trading on the markets, you are going to need to allow this Authentication. In most cases, you will need to download software onto your smartphone, such as Google Authenticator; however, some websites operate in a slightly different manner.

When you have successfully joined in to a large exchange website such as Poloniex or Kraken, you will be requested to input a code from your authenticator software. This code will be given to you when you have successfully logged in. These codes will be updated after each thirty second interval. Then, even if someone were to get your password, it would be useless after a period of thirty seconds. Additionally, two-factor authentication secures your withdrawals, which is an essential security feature. It will prompt you to provide a code once again if you are transferring money from an exchange into your wallet after moving them from the exchange.

If you did not set up a two-factor authentication system, it is possible for someone to steal your password, use it to access your account, and then walk or run away with all of your money while remaining completely unpunished. If you do not have the two-factor authentication, you are playing a risky game, and you will be the unfortunate one who loses. The reality of the matter is that there are a vast number of instances of victims posting on online forums and declaring that they had been hacked. They attribute it to unknown con artists operating in secrecy, one of whom may be an employee working for the exchange itself or possibly a sophisticated hacking team operating in another country.

If you have not established two-factor authentication, there is a genuine risk that someone will be able to get your security information and steal all of your money. This risk is increased if you have not implemented two-factor authentication. Install the two-factor authentication method before you deposit any money into any exchange.

The public has a great deal of curiosity around exchanges. What kind and how much money do you recommend I place in there? The majority of the advise that you will get will warn you to never leave money in the exchange; nevertheless, this piece of counsel does not make much sense since there is truly no purpose to keep them there anyhow. It is more prudent to keep complete control of your own keys.

Keep the money in that account until you reach the price you desire, if it ever occurs at all, given that you will want to trade. You have no way of knowing when that moment will arrive. It may be 10 days or it could be ten minutes. You will either have to decide to trade with an exchange that you can trust or give up trading altogether. Make an effort to distribute your cash among a number of different exchanges. Join five or six of such communities. Then, in the event that one of them is injured, they will not take you for all that you own.

Getting hacked and having all of your coins stolen is a terrible experience that causes a lot of suffering. There is no question about that. Nevertheless, the level of security has significantly improved over the course of these many years. Every significant exchange is aware that they need to recruit a large number of security engineers.

Conclude The Transaction And Move On.

Have you ever been in a position to sell anything, and as soon as the transaction is processed, you were overcome with feelings of remorse and worry? It's possible that you feel that you made the incorrect choice and passed up a significant opportunity for profit. Or, it's possible that you're anxious about the possibility that the little loss you sustained may have been transformed into a significant profit.

"There is always the next business opportunity. Stop dwelling on the mistake you made most recently and move on.

Now, smack dab in the midst of the trading day, you have to halt everything else you are doing so that you can monitor that one foolish play to make sure it really does go the way you thought it would when you sold. This is because you sold the stock based on your expectation that it would move in a certain direction. When it ticks the wrong way, it makes you feel terrible, and when it corrects itself, it makes you feel a little bit better. You are stuck in an unrelenting condition of emotional anguish all the time.

If you spend your time fixating on past failures, you increase the likelihood that you will have other failures in the future.

One error that I have made many times in the past, and that I see a lot of other players doing, is the tendency of believing that you have to earn that money back in the same play after you have suffered a significant loss. Due to the fact that you do not have a strong feel for the trade, it is possible that you will continue to make the same errors that caused you to lose money in the first place. Most of the time, it is best to move on to something else without carrying all of the emotional baggage that comes along with double down on a play that was unsuccessful.

If you are still licking your wounds from the last play, the chances will be stacked against you in the current transaction. However, if you are looking forward to the opportunity to use your abilities and convert them into a profit, then you have nothing to worry about.

When I exit a transaction that isn't profitable, I remove the corresponding ticker from my watch list. This keeps me from being tempted to re-enter the market and try to recoup the money that I've lost. Go invest your money on something new, pristine, and ideally something that's on the cutting edge of fashion.

Investing in NFTs

The purchasing and selling takes done on specialized platforms just for NFTs. Because there are many distinct categories of non-fungible tokens

(NFTs), such as art NFTs, trading card NFTs, and virtual land, to mention just a few, there are many distinct specialized platforms whose primary function is to process transactions for specific NFTs. In addition to these major NFT marketplaces, there are also a number of secondary markets where you are able to resell any NFT that you have acquired from a primary market. Therefore, before you pick a marketplace that is suitable for your NFT transactions, you need to think about the kind of non-fiat currency transaction that you intend to do.

Let's have a look at a variety of very recognized main and secondary markets for non-fungible tokens (NFTs).

Open water

Because it was released in 2018, this platform has the distinction of being the very first decentralized NFT marketplace in the NFT industry. The platform markets itself as the world's biggest marketplace for digital products, and it allows users to buy, sell, and trade a wide variety of one-of-a-kind digital goods and services. These one-of-a-kind products may be anything, from in-game items and domain names to collectibles and even digital representations of actual assets, such as a car or house. The platform is essentially the NFT equivalent of eBay in that it holds countless assets that are neatly categorized and arranged into hundreds of different categories, and it also enables its users to go to other NFT markets via the site itself.

Rare and hard to find

Alex Salnikov and Alexei Falin came up with the idea for this platform before it went live in the beginning of 2020. The platform is headquartered at Moscow. The network is designed specifically as a market for creative assets; nevertheless, users are permitted to exchange a wide variety of digital items on the platform. Users of the site have the ability, in addition to engaging in the trade of NFTs, to mint their very own NFTs. In case you were unaware, minting refers to the act of turning anything digital into a non-fungible token (NFT). Because of this, the network has attracted a large number of content producers who have begun minting NFTs based on their music albums, movies, songs, and other forms of media, and then selling these items via the platform.

In addition to the option of minting, content providers have the choice of either providing prospective purchasers with access to the whole content of their NFT or merely providing them with a preview of the material before revealing the complete content only once the NFT has been acquired in its entirety. Rarible, on the other hand, was forced to develop a verification procedure after coming across a few con artists who were attempting to sell false projects. This procedure allows Rarible to reduce the likelihood of its consumers having to deal with fraudulent projects.

Up to this point, the platform has been successful in luring in excess of 37,000 traders and has accomplished the goal of effectively generating $79.84 million in trading volume. The site has also attracted a few of major players, one of whom is LinseyLohan, who not only has a profile on the platform but also sold her own non-fungible token invention, Bitcoin Lightening, for little over $50,000 in what was one of the company's most lucrative transactions.

Nifty Gateway

The Winklevoss Twins, Tyler and Cameron, are responsible for the acquisition of Nifty Gateway, which is a platform that was first developed and released in 2018 by The Cock Foster Twins. The platform makes it possible to buy virtual products, which they call Nifties, and it also enables the purchase of Nifties for well-known crypto-games and apps like Gods Unchained and CryptoKitties.

One of the elements that contributes to the platform's popularity in the NFT arena is how simple it is to make purchases of NFTs on the platform. Buying an NFT on the platform is as easy as navigating to the marketplace on the platform using your web browser, selecting a product, entering your credit card information, and clicking the buy button. After making your purchase, you will be given the option to either save the newly acquired NFT in your Nifty Gateway account or transfer it to a wallet of your choosing.

You are need to submit an application before you will be granted permission to sell your own products on the site, despite the fact that it is easy to do so. A further feature of the site enables creators to decide the royalty rates that will apply to their works. As a result, the creator will get the defined rate anytime one of their products is resold.

Will The Price Of Cryptocurrency Continue To Soar?

The emergence of cryptocurrencies bears striking parallels to the dot-com boom of the late 1990s. In point of fact, many individuals have made the conscious decision to steer clear of cryptocurrencies because they do not want to repeat the mistakes made during the bursting of the dot-com boom.

Now, let's look at cryptocurrencies in light of the dot-com bubble to determine whether or not those people are correct to do so.

approximately April 1997 marked the beginning of the dot-com boom, and approximately June 2003 marked its collapse.

A bubble is a phenomenon that occurs in the business world when the price of an asset that can be freely exchanged in a well-established market rapidly increases, and then plummets and crashes over a period of time at rates that are inconsistent with what was reasonably expected to be realised by the investor who chose to own or hold the asset. In other words, the investor who chose to own or hold the asset should have expected to realise a certain return on their investment.

Consequently, if I were to approach you right now and say, "Hey! This scrap of paper is only worth one dollar right now, but in just five years it will be worth two hundred times that amount. If everyone else is purchasing it, you shouldn't hesitate to do so either.

You then make the decision to purchase it since you are concerned

about your financial situation (who isn't?).

Six months later, the value of the paper starts to quickly increase; something that you purchased for a dollar a unit is now selling for $50, and you are pleased with this development.

In your capacity as a shrewd investor, you have decided to keep the paper in your possession because you anticipate that during the next several months, it will be valued at least $100 per unit.

The next day, you go to sleep, and when you wake up, you find out that the value of your valuable paper has plummeted overnight.

You start having trouble selling them, and by the time you do find someone who is willing to take them off your hands, they are only willing to pay fifty cents for each paper.

This is precisely what occurred during the era of the dot-com bubble. At the time, the internet was a relatively new and developing innovation, and many people felt that it was going to have a significant influence on society and eventually take control of the whole globe (well, they weren't exactly wrong, were they?)

Therefore, investors started purchasing a significant amount of stock in online companies with the hope of making a profit when the expansion of the internet market began to provide some revenue.

However, they failed to take into account the fact that the majority of the online firms in which they were investing had few physical assets; as a result, these companies were simply overpriced, which caused many market analysts to lose their jobs when the market collapsed.

There are a lot of parallels to be seen between the dot-com bubble and the current situation in the cryptocurrency business, and one does not need to be an expert in economics to recognise these parallels.

Bitcoin, the first cryptocurrency, began trading in 2009 for nearly nothing. This was when it initially started trading. According to legend, one of the first people to invest in bitcoin spent 10,000 BTC at one point in history to place an indirect order with Papa John's for two pizza delivery.

However, one bitcoin is now worth thousands of dollars, representing a significant growth percentage in only a few short years. This phenomenon is comparable to the dot-com boom.

In today's cryptocurrency business, there is also something of a frenzy around initial coin offerings (ICOs). Initial Coin Offering is an unregulated method of raising capital for a new cryptocurrency endeavour (the launch of a new kind of coin). This method is also referred to as an ICO.

People are investing in several cryptocurrencies exactly as they did during the dotcom era, when many new internet firms were emerging and people were investing in them; abandoning their jobs to become full-time traders. This is similar to the situation that existed during the dotcom era.

You wouldn't be incorrect if you dubbed the cryptocurrency revolution a bubble and compared it

to the dot-com boom. However, here are some reasons why comparing the cryptocurrency revolution to the dot-com bubble is naive and excessively simple.

If you look closely at the dot-com period, specifically the reasons why the bubble burst, you'll see that everything came tumbling down long before the industry had developed to a stage of maturity where it could create actual profits to support the high valuations that existed shortly before the bubble burst. This is because the business had not yet reached the point where it could generate genuine profits to justify the high valuations.

If you look at firms like Google, Microsoft, and Amazon as well as other progeny of the internet like Facebook, Netflix, and others, you'll notice that the forecasts were not entirely off the mark because these companies have grown to be quite valuable today. Other examples include Facebook and Netflix.

At today's exchange rates, Google's market worth is around $680 billion, while Microsoft's is approximately $540 billion, and Facebook's is approximately $478 billion.

It indicates that the forecasts made regarding dotcoms, which resulted in a frenzy of investment and propelled the market higher, were not entirely inaccurate.

It is true that many dot-com firms failed, but the reason for their failures was not because the dot-com innovation was a stupid concept (just as the technology behind blockchain is not a stupid idea), nor was it because investing in the industry was not going to be successful ultimately. It was due to the fact that investors chose to ignore a variety of factors, such as the fact that the internet was still a new invention and too young to produce earnings to justify the high P/E ratio being credited to dotcom stocks at the time (some as high as a 200 P/E ratio). This was one of the primary reasons why the dotcom bubble burst.

Investors who made shrewd investments at that time and had the patience to wait for a new invention to mature before placing too high of an expectation on its potential return wouldn't exactly refer to the dotcom period as a bubble.

Although it is true that we are witnessing some of the same patterns in the cryptocurrency business today, such as the daily birth of initial coin offerings

(ICOs) and new currencies, as well as over-speculation, this phenomenon is not unique to the cryptocurrency market and can occur in any market.

How Does The Operation Of Cryptocurrencies Work?

The world of cryptocurrencies is often seen as confusing and cloaked in secrecy by the general public. In the following paragraphs, I will throw some light on this enigma by describing how cryptocurrency transactions take place. You need to get familiar with the following eight essential ideas, which form the backbone of most cryptocurrency networks, in order to comprehend how cryptocurrencies function. These concepts are listed in alphabetical order.

A code or cypher

The term "encryption" refers to the process of converting data or information into an unbreakable code with the purpose of securing it from being viewed by unauthorised parties. The most reliable method of protecting sensitive information is known as encryption. A person who does not have access to the secret key that is necessary to decode the file is unable to read the encrypted file.

Encryption is the primary method through which cryptocurrency transactions are protected. Cryptocurrencies, in contrast to other types of encryption that rely on a single key for both encryption and decryption, employ two distinct keys for each operation: encryption and decryption. When a user conducts a transaction, a pair of keys that are mathematically linked together is produced. These keys consist of a private key and a public key. The data is encrypted using the public key, and the private key is needed in order to decode the information.

The address of the bitcoin wallet may be derived from the public key. Anyone in possession of the address has the ability to transfer bitcoin units (information that has been encrypted) to another user on the network. It is necessary to have the associated private key in order to decode this information.

A move away from centralised control

One of the defining features of cryptocurrencies is their decentralised nature, which also happens to be one of their primary advantages. The act of transferring the authority to make choices, perform activities, and take responsibility for the outcomes from a centralised authority is referred to as decentralisation. After then, responsibilities are assigned to specific individuals or groups within the organisation and disseminated to them. In a bitcoin network, all of the computers share the responsibility for performing the necessary operations.

The blockchain technology that underpins cryptocurrencies is essentially a protocol, not unlike the internet. Because of this, it is impossible for a single person to assert control over a coin. To create a cryptocurrency, certain mathematical criteria have to be followed. After then, these guidelines are obligatory for all users. For example, there is no centralised body that monitors the transactions that take place with cryptocurrencies. Instead, in order for a transaction to be confirmed, it is necessary for all of the computers that are part of the network to concur that it has taken place.

Systems That Are Distributed

A software application known as a distributed system is one that is stored on a large number of separate and independent machines that are all linked together to form a network. These computers are able to communicate with one another and work together to achieve a common objective by coordinating their operations. Platforms for cryptocurrencies are decentralised, distributed systems. A cryptocurrency platform utilises numerous computers all at once to carry out its operations. This indicates that the network will continue to function normally even if one of the computers on the network is taken down since the other computers on the network will step in to fill the void.

Free and Public Source Code

This term refers to computer programmes in which the source code is made available to the general public without charge. Anyone is free to look at, alter, and distribute the source code without having to pay any kind of charge. The development of open source software is assisted by a large number of individuals.

Because cryptocurrencies are distributed using an open-source model, anybody has the ability to freely use them, alter their code, or establish Application Protocol Interfaces (APIs).

Business dealings

The moving of units of a cryptocurrency from one digital wallet to another is what's referred to as a transaction in the world of cryptocurrencies. A single encrypted data structure is produced by the digital wallet client whenever a bitcoin transaction is carried out. After then, the data structure in question is recorded in a public ledger, where it awaits confirmation. The mathematical evidence of the transaction's completion is provided by the sender's wallet, which was sent along with the bitcoins. The transaction is sent to other computers on the network so that it can be redistributed. When all of the computers agree that the transaction is legitimate, it is added to the public ledger so that it will be there indefinitely.

There are three components that make up a transaction. The first component is an input, and it requires the public address of the sender. The quantity of units of the cryptocurrency that are being transmitted is the second component. The public address of the receiver is the third component, which is referred to as an output. For the purpose of signing the transaction, the sender will utilise his or her private key. It is important to keep in mind that a cryptocurrency wallet does not actually receive or store any coins themselves. Instead, it stores the secure digital (private) key that is necessary to sign transactions and access the public cryptocurrency wallet address. This key is contained within the wallet itself.

The Bitcoin programme is available for anybody to use. This indicates that anyone is able to not only examine the source code but also copy it and make modifications to their own copy in order to produce something completely original. That is precisely how a significant number of the alternative cryptocurrencies, sometimes known as "altcoins," that are covered in this book came into being. The earliest of these Bitcoin offshoots, and for a while the most popular of them all, is called Litecoin.

Litecoin is a cryptocurrency that uses many of the same principles as Bitcoin but improves upon them. Charles Lee, who is the brother of Bobby Lee, the president of BTC China, which is one of the top Bitcoin and Litecoin exchanges in China, was the first person to publish it. His goal was to develop a superior alternative to the cryptocurrency known as Bitcoin. The end consequence was the creation of a new digital currency, which some people consider to be the silver to Bitcoin's gold.

The underlying architecture of Bitcoin was enhanced in a number of ways by Litecoin. The hashing algorithm that was utilised for the purpose of verifying transactions on the blockchain underwent a significant transformation. You may recall from the prior chapter that "miners" are the nodes that are responsible for adding new blocks of transactions to the blockchain. A payment will be given to the first miner (or group of miners) who is able to solve a difficult mathematical issue. All of these miners are vying against one another to find a solution to the challenge. The SHA-256 encryption technique underpins the mathematical calculations that are carried out in Bitcoin transactions. While it is not necessary for end users to have any knowledge of SHA-256, it is necessary for us to go a bit further than the typical user in order to comprehend the rationale behind the existence of Litecoin.

It was fairly simple to configure devices specifically for the purpose of mining Bitcoin using SHA-256, which was a significant shortcoming in terms of accessibility and decentralisation. The first dedicated Bitcoin mining devices, which were specialised computers that did nothing but do SHA-256 computations, began to appear on the market not long after Bitcoin gained popularity. When it came to mining Bitcoin, these specialised miners were far more effective than even the most powerful personal PCs. Soon after, the installation of a large number of these miners began to concentrate administration of the Bitcoin network into a limited number of full-time operations, whose only goal is the verification of Bitcoin blocks in order to reap the benefits. This trend is expected to continue in the foreseeable future.

You may remember from the Bitcoin chapter that the decentralised nature of Bitcoin is one of its most notable characteristics. Some people believed that the concentration of mining was such a significant risk that it was necessary to establish an alternative currency in order to protect themselves from it.

By employing a new hashing method, Litecoin makes an effort to circumvent the aforementioned problem. This technique, which is known as Scrypt, relies on the memory of the device rather than the processing speed of the device. Mining blocks is now a more feasible activity for the typical player as a result of this development, which decreases the need to construct enormous mining farms.

Litecoin transactions were also verified at a far faster pace than Bitcoin ones. Whereas the algorithms used by Bitcoin solve a block on average every ten minutes, the Scrypt algorithm used by Litecoin solves a block about every two and a half minutes. This results in a significantly increased rate of transaction processing speed compared to the alternative. The Litecoin network generates four times as many currency units every block as the Bitcoin network does. This is done so that the network can compensate for the quicker block processing.

The fact that Litecoin has achieved its primary objective of being more efficient than Bitcoin is one of the things that makes it such an intriguing cryptocurrency. It is now ranked among the top five cryptocurrencies in terms of market capitalisation, trailing only Bitcoin and Ethereum by a somewhat small margin. This is likely the most accurate representation of what the Litecoin project aimed to accomplish. Its purpose wasn't to create havoc on the market; rather, it was to function as a more advantageous alternative to the dominant currency. Litecoin did not provide any fundamental changes to the cryptocurrency industry, but it did enhance the way in which cryptocurrencies may be used. The specifications of Litecoin are different from those of Bitcoin, yet many consider these changes to be improvements. Regardless, it is now the most viable alternative to Bitcoin for making straightforward monetary transactions, as measured by its market cap. Over the course of the past year, the price of Litecoin has skyrocketed from $4 to $80.

Mining For Bitcoin In The Cloud

There is an alternative to consider if you are interested in investing in Bitcoin mining but do not want the hassle of managing your own hardware. You may put the cloud to work for you and bring in some coin. To put it more simply, cloud mining refers to the practise of utilising pooled processing power that is managed by a remote data centre. One needs nothing more than a computer at home for communication, a local Bitcoin wallet (though this is optional), and so on.

However, before making a purchase, potential buyers need to be aware of some risks associated with cloud mining. These risks might affect the profitability of the investment.

PROS

The following are some of the reasons why you should think about cloud mining:

A calmer and more comfortable home - no fan that is always humming

There is no additional cost for electricity.

When mining stopped being economical, there was no equipment left to sell.

There are no ventilation issues with the hot equipment.

Less likelihood of being disappointed by mining equipment vendors.

CONS

The following are some of the reasons why you should probably avoid cloud mining:

Possibility of fraud

Lower earnings due to fewer operations since the operators, in the end, need to make enough money to cover their expenses.

Contractual warnings that mining operationsmayceasedependingon the priceofBitcoin

Lackofcontrol and flexibility.

DIFFERENT METHODS OF CLOUD MINING

The following are the three primary types of remote gambling that may be played at the moment:

Leasing a mining machine that is hosted by the provider You can lease a mining machine that is hosted by the provider.

Create a (general purpose) virtual private server, then install your own mining software on that server. This is known as "virtually hosted mining."

power was allowed to be wasted

Allow a certain level of hashing power to be used without the need for a dedicated real or virtual machine. (This is by a significant margin the most used approach of cloud mining.)

The Advantages Of Engaging In Currency Trading

There is a plethora of justification for you to give some thought to purchasing the currency. Some of these reasons include the following:

Entry requirements: There are virtually no barriers to entry into the bitcoin market, in contrast to the stock market and other trading channels. Identifying a vendor from whom you may make a purchase is all that is required of you at this point. If you are interested in selling, all you need to do is find a buyer, and you will be all set.

Global: You are able to engage in currency trade from any location on the planet. This indicates that a person in China may purchase Bitcoin from or sell Bitcoin to a person in Africa or any other part of the world. As a result, the value of the currency has increased significantly, and it is no longer dependent on the economy of a single nation.

It is subject to change: Bitcoin, like the other currencies traded on the foreign exchange market, is subject to significant price swings. This indicates that its price shifts rapidly in response to even minute shifts in the state of the economy. If you capitalise on the opportunities presented by the shifts, you might realise enormous profits.

24-hour-a-day trading: Trading in bitcoin takes place throughout the day and night, in contrast to the stock market, which only operates during business hours. You are the only one who is restricted in terms of trading—not time.

How to locate a source for the virtual currency known as bitcoin

If you are interested in entering the market, there are several different methods that you may obtain the cash that you will need. You may use it in a variety of ways, including the following:

When buying on an exchange, you should: You will find people in this area that are interested in selling the currency if you go into the marketplace as soon as possible. You should search for a trustworthy vendor and then make an order with them.

Transfer: Another way to get Bitcoin is through a friend's exchange. A friend will need to send you the currency through an application that may be found on a computer or a mobile device.

This is the traditional method for obtaining the coins, known as "mining." Using this approach, you will solve difficult mathematical conundrums with the assistance of a computer. You are given the coins as a prise whenever you solve a puzzle to the best of your ability. Although this approach doesn't cost anything, it might take quite a bit of time to complete.

The Market

One of the least obvious characteristics of contemporary economics is the way in which prices on the market are related to individuals' perceptions of what something is worth. It may be thought of as the relationship between subjective valuations and objective monetary values. When discussing the subjective nature of the issue, there is no one unit of measurement that can be used.

People are able to evaluate and categorise items in accordance with their own preferences by assigning values to those commodities. Within the realm of management theory, the idea of value creation is an essential component.

The word "marketplace" can have two different meanings depending on context. To begin, a marketplace refers to a physical location, such as a supermarket, a shopping mall, or a car dealership, where individuals may go to sell, purchase, or exchange a product or item. However, a marketplace can also be digital, and examples of such platforms include Amazon, eBay, Alibaba, Shopify, and many more. Second, the word "market" or "marketplace" can also be used to refer to the presence of individuals who are interested in purchasing, selling, or exchanging a specific kind of good or service. There is a market for a certain product in which it is possible to arouse desire and tailor the product to the preferences or tastes of consumers.

Various organisational strategies may be used to organise a market, including the following:

Free competition takes place when consumers have the ability to select from a variety of various offerings and the price of an item or service is determined by the interaction of several bids from competing businesses for that good or service.

Oligopoly is a situation in which a limited number of operators make offers to customers.

The condition known as monopoly arises when there is no other option except to accept the price that is being offered.

The emergence of the free market has resulted in a multitude of positive outcomes for communal life. In market research and marketing, the requirements of consumers and the value they place on various goods or services are consistently brought to the forefront. This interpretation of the phrase is significantly more philosophical: When a large number of individuals have an interest in purchasing or selling a certain good, service, piece of information, or money, a market has formed.

The link between the amount of items that are accessible and the order is what determines the market value of any and all tangible assets. This is because supply and demand are directly proportional to one another. In the world of physical assets, there is a concept of scarcity of support, which is not present in the world of digital assets and has not been for a very long time. A purchase that is available in large quantities or in total, even if it is highly desired, does not acquire value because those who seek to possess it can easily obtain it. As an illustration, an asset that is highly sought after but scarce gains value as a result of the competition between those who want it.

A company will conduct a market test in order to determine the sorts of customers who will be interested in purchasing a product before it is released to the public. This test assists businesses in determining the amount of money customers are willing to spend in order to acquire their items. The findings indicate that different people have an interest in various things and are willing to spend a given price for a specific commodity. These days, businesses pay attention to what their customers want and work to fulfil those requirements. The idea of scarcity, which has always been the foundation of classical economics, is what often determines pricing and places the primary emphasis on goods that meet the needs of 80 percent of the population. The proliferation of options may be directly attributed to the advent of the internet. Due to the fact that it is accessible to people all over the world, the internet provides larger business opportunities. This means that virtually every product or item may locate its target audience online. "The long tail" is a retail concept that is based on statistical research, and it was Chris Anderson's desire to implement this approach. It is more profitable for a business to offer a wide variety of one-of-a-kind goods in a limited quantity than it is to sell a select few popular items in a huge quantity.

On the internet, there are seldom any middlemen to be found in the market. Therefore, trust and views passed through verbally are quite important, and they represent the most cutting-edge means of marketing available on the internet.

Ways That One Can Make Money Using Cryptocurrency

Buying and selling bitcoin assets according to a set of predetermined guidelines is an element of a trading strategy.

A solid trading strategy should contain a well-thought-out plan that outlines particular trading objectives, a trading period, and a risk tolerance plan. This plan should also be documented.

The strategy calls for the creation of procedures that are aimed at the purchase and sale of crypto assets. It should also include a plan that satisfies the objectives you have set for your investments. Trading techniques are useful tools for determining where to enter and leave the cryptocurrency market.

Strategies for Investing in Virtual Currencies

Buy and hold on to it.

Buy and hold, also known as HODL, is the most fundamental trading method, in which you purchase the crypto asset, keep it for a period of time, and then eventually sell it. It takes a significant amount of faith to keep holding onto the asset. Holding on to an asset with the hopes of selling it at a profit at a later date requires you to have confidence that the price will continue to rise. As long as the prices are going up, the investor will keep holding onto the asset. The buy-and-hold investment strategy benefits from a rising market.

The buy-and-hold investing strategy for cryptocurrencies is denoted by the term "HODL," which stands for "Hold On

ForDear Life." This term has become popular in the Bitcoin crypto-sphere. Keeping the coin in one's possession for a predetermined amount of time might result in long-term rewards for cryptocurrency traders.

Many investors who hold on to their holdings for as long as possible have been successful in meeting their long-term business objectives. One strategy to reduce exposure to risk while investing is to spread your money over a number of different digital currencies, such as Ethereum, EOS, Ripple, and others.

The profits that may be made from investing in higher-priced cryptocurrencies are not as significant as those that can be made from investing in lower-priced cryptocurrencies. At this moment in time, an investor may purchase nearly 50 Ethereum for the same price as one Bitcoin. This difference can vary, but at its highest point, it was almost 20:1 when comparing the prices of Bitcoin and Ethereum. Better returns on the bitcoin portfolio may be achieved through diversification, which also helps to re-balance the portfolio.

The majority of investors who use the buy-and-hold strategy do not implement a stop-loss, which would trigger a sell order if the price decreased by an amount that would make the investor feel uneasy. Setting a stop-loss order, on the other hand, eliminates the element of emotion from trading. It is impossible to recover from the loss, but it saves the investor from suffering an even worse loss. Successful investors typically advise others to use stop-loss orders to reduce their exposure to losses.

4.A Mining Strategy and Plan

The starter-pack is almost finished being assembled. The next thing you'll need is a mining programme or software, which is a piece of computer code that will solve mathematical puzzles in order to earn money for you. You will need to establish a connection between this and the pool of your choosing. In order for the programme to function correctly, it is typically necessary to have a batch file or a series of commands to follow.

BFGminer and CGminer are two of the most well-liked mining programmes available today. Both of these applications are run through the command line.

5.A Computer That Is Exclusively Used for Mining

It's possible that after spending so much money on the first two items on this list, your bank account is already warning you to slow down and cut back on your spending. However, the mining process does require its own dedicated computer system in order to function properly. This occurs because, as soon as your mining programme begins operating, all of the other tasks being performed on your computer become extremely sluggish and eventually come to a complete halt.

If you wish to begin receiving "newly minted" coins via a proof-of-work system, you will first need to have those things in your possession. It is my hope that you have not overlooked the fact that it is necessary to continue the discussion on the needs for the system's equivalent.

Considerations Regarding The Pros And Cons Of Using Cryptocurrencies

There are benefits and drawbacks to using cryptocurrencies, despite the fact that their popularity is at an all-time high. These pros and cons will help businesspeople decide what factors are most important to take into consideration. The following are some of the benefits that cryptocurrencies offer:

It is not possible to take possession of cryptocurrencies such as Bitcoin. This is because ledgers are used to record the transactions that take place. There are more than one and two of these ledgers. Multiple versions of the transactions are kept on file. Because of this, it is far more difficult to steal cryptocurrency.

There are currently no taxes imposed on cryptocurrencies. This is due to the fact that they are self-sufficient. One and only choice a person has is whether or not to increase the amount of money being sent in as taxes. But no one can get away with taxing cryptocurrencies because of their decentralized nature.

Everything that goes on between parties has been labeled 'confidential.' This ensures that nobody can find out how much money a person has. Neither of them can determine how much money has been exchanged between them.

Because of their confidentiality and anonymity, they are difficult to steal.

Making payments is a simple process. They are completed more quickly. The answer to this question will be determined by the type of cryptocurrency that they have chosen to utilize. A block may take some people thirty seconds to complete. One moment, please, others.

In spite of these benefits, there are a number of drawbacks associated with them.

Once a transaction is completed, there is no way to undo it. Cryptocurrencies, in contrast to banks, which allow transactions to be canceled, do not support this functionality. This indicates that people need to pay close attention to the particulars. Accidentally entering the wrong information could result in the loss of the entire transaction.

There are certain countries that limit or prohibit the usage of them. The amount that can be purchased and the services that can be used are both subject to restrictions.

Because of their anonymity, their use may be contrary to the law. In most instances, they could lead to the exchange of illegal substances. Others would be able to use them to virtually purchase armor with them.

It's possible to misplace your wallet. This is especially true in the event that a PC crashes.

Their values don't stay the same very often. They move up and down according to how the market is doing.

The Technology BehindBlockchain

The very first cryptocurrency that was ever made official.Blockchain technology, which is what Bitcoin is built on, is responsible for the decentralization of the transaction process. The blockchain is a distributed public ledger that uses the 'hash' for anonymity, the 'proof of work' idea for maintaining correct transaction management, and offers incentives for confirming the transactions that have been initiated. If all of these aspects, including the hash, the proof of work, and the incentives (for currency production), work together, then it will be possible to properly apply the blockchain technology.

What precisely is the Blockchain?

The blockchain technology follows the concept of decentralization, which involves verifying and updating all of the transactions in a distributed public ledger. This means that every single entity in the network maintains a copy of all of the transactions that have ever occurred in the history of the blockchain network. This is in contrast to the concept of a central database or ledger that is used in traditional banking transactions. If an entity tries to change the transaction, then it will not match the original block, which is already updated in the single ledger of every entity in the network. This notion makes it impossible to tamper with the transactional data since it prevents an entity from successfully changing the transaction. Therefore, when a hash algorithm is executed, the difference that exists between the original hash value and the new hash of the modified transaction block becomes apparent, which in turn causes the block to be marked as 'fake.'

The mode of the transaction can be traced, but the identity of the account will never be known as all of the data in the blockchain is encrypted using the hash algorithm, and it is almost impossible to decrypt the data because even a minor change in the input will generate a different hash that is completely unrelated to the original hash. This is because even a minute change in the input will generate a different hash. After the 'proof of work' (cryptographic problem) has been completed successfully, the transaction request will be able to be confirmed.

When a new transaction request is issued in the network, all of the requests are compiled into a single block. The miners then work together to determine the hash that will validate the transactions, stamp the transactions, and then add them to the chain that is already in existence, so validating the transaction. The transaction data, a hash, and a Nonce are the components that make up a block of transactions. In order to solve the hash, the miners make use of the proof of work, or PoW, and if they are successful, they are rewarded with cryptocurrency. Miners in the Bitcoin network are rewarded with 12.5 bitcoins for each transaction block that they create that is validated successfully. The typical amount of time spent mining a Bitcoin block is ten minutes, however on the Ethereum network, same process takes only fifteen seconds. This time gap changes depending on the individual coins that are being discussed.

A public-distributed database that contains encrypted ledgers and blocks that record the most recent transaction constitutes the blockchain. This database is accessible to the public. After the block has been checked for accuracy, it is added to the already existing chain of blocks, making it an irreversible component of the blockchain. Therefore, if there is a request for a transaction (one person transferring Bitcoin to another person), it instantly gets added to the blockchain with a'specific code' (hash), and it is then broadcast to every other entity that is a part of the Bitcoin network. After the miner has successfully validated the transaction request by solving the Proof-of-Work problem, he will then add the newly validated transaction block to the previously established blockchain, thereby making the change permanent.

The transaction is considered finalized once this step is carried out because the recipient is then given the Bitcoin. The miner is rewarded 12.5 bitcoins for completing this particular operation, which is known as the mining process.

In his white papers, Satoshi Nakamoto gives the following definition of the blockchain: "a peer-to-peer electronic cash system, which helps in enabling 'online transactions to be done directly between the sender and recipient without the necessity of an intermediary."

How exactly does it function?

When a new transaction request is made, the previous ones are collected together into a block, which is then protected by a 'hash' that is generated by a cryptographic algorithm. This block is then broadcast to the entire cryptocurrency network every ten minutes, based on the flow of transactions. After the miners in the network have worked to validate the transaction by solving the hash using PoW (proof of work), the blocks that have been successfully validated are stamped, and then they are added to the blockchain in the order of linear chronological precedence. This shows every single transaction that has ever taken place in the history of the blockchain, and it is continually updated to match every single ledger that is part of the network. The blockchain is organized in the form of a chain, and each new transaction block is continually added to the previous blocks in this style.

Because the blockchain technology follows a safe encrypted and decentralized procedure, it is impossible to hack the blockchain, which in turn raises the level of trust that exists between peers. This in turn makes it impossible to steal cryptocurrency from the blockchain. If a hacker wants to break into a specific transaction block, he will first need to validate the hash of that block, which requires him to have the hash of the block that came before it. This, in turn, will require the hash of the block that came before it, which will require the hacker to solve the hash of the entire blockchain, which is utterly unachievable due to the fact that the figure willexceed'millions.'

A brief summary of the mining process is as follows:

This transaction block is then validated by solving the "complex algorithms," and when it is successfully verified, they are added to the existing blocks. - The transaction request is begun, which is then broadcasted to the entire network (P2P – peer to peer network). - When the transaction request is successfully verified, it is added to the existing blocks.

These transaction requests can be cryptocurrencies or contracts (smart contracts in the case of Ethereum), or any other information depending on the crypto coin and its platform. - The new verified transaction block is now included to the existing blockchain, thereby creating a new data block for the ledger (updating in the distributed ledger) - The crypto coin and its platform determine the type of information that can be included in these transaction requests. It is now impossible to change or edit the data in the blockchain because the newly added block has become an integral and permanent part of the chain. The transaction request that was started has now been finished, which means that its status has changed from "pending" to "successful."

Binance Coin

A cryptocurrency that originates from the Binance ecosystem is called Binance coin. Binance is a cryptocurrency exchange that gives its customers the ability to buy, sell, and trade in whatever cryptocurrency they want. As the largest cryptocurrency exchange in the world, it was initially built on Ethereum'sblockchain and now operates on its own blockchain, which is simply called Binance chain.

Users have the option of paying the withdrawal charge that is incurred when moving their cryptocurrency away from the Binance exchange and into their personal wallets by using Binance coins, also known as BNB. BNB was developed as a means of funding the expansion of the exchange as well as rewarding users for their continued devotion to the platform. It has evolved to the point where that restricted scope is no longer enough. Users are able to pay for hotel reservations and flight bookings with the token in various use cases, such as when they book flights. On some platforms, you are able to use it to make stock investments. You also have the option to swap Binance coins for a variety of other cryptocurrencies. Changpeng Zhao was the one who came up with the idea on July 21st, 2017.

After two years, in April of 2019, the cryptocurrency exchange platform finally debuted its Binance Chain. This was the very first chain to implement a whole new protocol that was referred to as decentralized exchanges. Decentralization is simply taken and applied to the platform of a cryptocurrency exchange in this method. Because of this, decentralized cryptocurrency exchanges came into existence. In the language of cryptocurrencies, this type of exchange is known as a DEX. Because a user does not even need to give out personal information to the exchange in order to engage in the realm of digital money, they bring freedom to a whole new level. Users are able to establish a direct connection to the distributed ledger network. The decentralized exchange does not experience problems with downtime since it operates utilizing nodes, which are computers located in various locations throughout the world. It was designed from the ground up to provide decentralized trade at lightning-fast speeds. The Binance Chain and the Binance DEX were developed to make the process of trading assets, which is traditionally carried out on controlled exchanges, more efficient. You might be wondering what problem this will actually solve. Having said that, taking into consideration the fact that a big number of individuals are now getting involved with cryptocurrencies, the load that is being placed on the system is only going to increase. Exchanges are highly vital to the proper functioning of everything in this world because they are the only platform available to enter it. It is not able to tolerate any kind of delays, lags, or crashes. Decentralizing these interactions is a straightforward concept, but carrying it out will be a challenging endeavor. Binance Chain is an invention that addresses this issue and comes into play here. After the launch of Binance Chain, BNB was designated as the platform's native coin. It originated on the blockchain of Ethereum and was later migrated.

Binance'sBinance Smart Chain was released into the wild on September 1st,

2020. It does it in a manner similar to that of the Binance Chain. Users are able to create smart contracts on the smart chain that are comparable to those that are possible on the Ethereumblockchain. This new blockchain is consistent with the decentralized financial revolution that is taking place through the cryptocurrency economy. DeFi is an exciting new frontier that is made feasible by cryptos and holds great potential. There is a great deal of potential for it in the years to come. In addition to this, the Smart Chain is capable of processing a new block in approximately three seconds! In addition to this, basing the blockchain on a proof-of-stake method makes it possible to reduce the amount of electricity required to maintain it, making it an ecologically friendly alternative similar to Ethereum. In order to take part in the validation of transactions on this blockchain, participants are required to stake some BNB. They do this in exchange for a reward, which comes in the form of transaction fees. The supply of the Binance coin, which is deflationary in nature, will gradually decline over time, just like Bitcoin does. In order to accomplish this, the core team that is in charge of running the platform makes use of a technique known as coin burning. It is a means of "burning" certain coins from the total amount that are in circulation, which is exactly what the name says it is. The data on the number of trades carried out over the preceding three months was used to calculate the total number of coins that were burned. Every three months, a total of one hundred million BNB are destroyed by burning Binance coins. There have been a total of 200,000,000 BNB issued in circulation at this time. The destruction of half of the total coins in circulation ensures that the supply is kept under control. Because of this, the coin is an attractive investment opportunity from a financial point of view.

Burning coins requires the use of a function called "burn." It is a specialized form of an electronic contract. Burn is the initial operation that will be carried out by a coin holder. After that, the system examines the holder to see if they have a sufficient amount of coins. If this does not happen, the burn function will not be finished. If the person in question does possess coins, those coins will be obliterated permanently so that they are no longer part of the system. However, the blockchain will still include a record of this burn after it has occurred. A transaction is created and added to the blockchain whenever a burn occurs. Everyone is able to view the total number of coins that have been consumed, and the system itself is entirely open and accessible. Coin burns have been performed on a quarterly basis by the Binance team on a constant basis. They purchase from the market the necessary quantity of BNB to be destroyed and then destroy the BNB themselves. In April of 2021, the very last one was completed. There was a loss of around one million BNB, or 595 million dollars. This is a fresh take on the traditional ways of thinking about the demand, supply, and value of cryptocurrencies.

It is important to keep in mind that BNB is the token that powers the entirety of Binance's ecosystem, which includes its two parallel blockchains known as the Binance Chain and the Binance Smart Chain. This is an important point to keep in mind throughout all of this. At the time that BNB was first made available on the market, the exchange rate was 2700 BNB to 1 ETH. At first, the BNB ERC-20 token was utilized on the

Ethereum platform. Following the migration of Binance to its own Binance Chain, this was modified using a BNB BEP-2. As a result, there are three distinct types of BNB that are now in use and circulation inside the cryptocurrency ecosystem. BEP-2, BEP-20, and ERC-20 are all related. The first two are reserved for Binance chain transactions. The most recent one may be put to use on the Ethereum network. Therefore, what kinds of things can we do with a BNB? Aside from the usage of paying off transaction fees on Binance, which has already been stated, you may also use it to purchase products and services both online and in-store. You can accomplish this goal by using either a Binance card or Binance pay. To put it in the simplest terms, using it is exactly the same as using a credit card, with the exception that you pay with BNB rather than a traditional currency. You can now utilize BNB to make use of services made available to you by decentralized applications thanks to the smart chain that it possesses.

At the moment, one Bitcoin Cash can be purchased for 315 dollars. On the market at this time, there are approximately 153,432,897 Binance coins in circulation. It is now ranked number four on the list of the top ten companies based on market capitalization.

Mining for cryptocurrencies

Mining cryptocurrencies is an additional method of investing in this space. Before we get into the various methods of mining for cryptocurrencies, it is important that you first grasp the significance of mining and the environment in which it takes place. So why is it necessary to engage in mining activity? Mining is the process that is used to verify and process records or blocks. Without mining, no new records will be processed, and this will result in the addition of no new blocks to the blockchain. Mining is therefore regarded as being critically vital within the context of blockchain technology. Because of this, it is significant for bitcoin as well as other cryptocurrencies.

Since you are now aware of the significance of mining, we can go on to a discussion of the many ways in which cryptocurrencies can be mined:

Mining done on computers

The term "solo mining" refers to the most fundamental form of cryptocurrency mining, which entails mining digital assets only through the use of a personal computer. This is a simple task to complete. You can begin mining cryptocurrency by downloading mining software such as GUIMiner, connecting to a mining pool, and following the instructions provided by the mining pool. Nevertheless, the drawback of taking this strategy is that you won't even get close to earning a respectable amount of cryptocurrency. In point of fact, it is highly possible that the amount of money that you spend on energy will wind up being greater than the amount of cryptocurrency that you are really able to generate. The reason for this is that a single machine does not have the hash power to be able to mine additional coins by itself. Be wary when

160

using computer mining software because it might cause your computer to overheat, which is especially likely if you mine for long periods of time. If you mine for too long, your computer could overheat and possibly crash, so try to limit your sessions.

The mining of hardware

In order to mine a sufficient amount of cryptocurrency, some miners need specialized hardware in addition to mining using a computer. This is due to the fact that mining with a computer alone is not sufficient. This process is referred to as mining on hardware. The hardware will provide you with more mining power, allowing you to mine a greater quantity of cryptocurrency. It is important to keep in mind that even if you mine using specialized hardware, you will still need to make use of your computer. As a result, you still need to be vigilant regarding any overheating issues that may crop up in the future. Taking this strategy can be problematic for a number of reasons, one of which is that purchasing mining hardware of a high quality can be quite pricey.

Mining done on software

You can mine bitcoins by purchasing mining software and putting it to use. This is known as software mining. In addition, a software mining provider might make it possible for you to upgrade your mining software in exchange for a charge, which would enable you to mine more efficiently. Even if you do not need to utilize any specialized mining hardware, you will still need to mine cryptocurrency on your computer in order to run the necessary software.

Mining in the cloud

One of the most common approaches to mining in use today is known as cloud mining. Mining cryptocurrencies on your personal computer is no longer necessary thanks to the advent of cloud mining. You won't even need to buy mining software or gear to get started. Instead, you can hire a mining firm to take care of everything for you. All that is required of you at this point is to wait for the cryptocurrency to be sent to you by the mining firm. This may occur on a weekly basis or whenever your balance reaches a predetermined minimum level. There is, of course, a cost associated with using cloud mining services. After all, no cryptocurrency mining business worth their salt will work for you unless they stand to gain something in the process. The hitch is that in order for a mining firm to begin mining for you, you will need to pay them or invest money in the company first. To some, it might look like this: You can choose to invest or pay 0.7 Bitcoin to receive up to 0.013 Bitcoin weekly. Even though it may look like a fantastic offer, there is no guarantee that it actually is one. This is due to the fact that the amount that you believe you will receive from your broker is really an estimate, and not the amount that you can actually anticipate receiving from them. This indicates that if you use the example provided, you might receive as little as 0.005 BTC or even less than that.

Because of this, if you are going to participate in cloud mining, you should only work with a mining firm that is reputable and trustworthy.

A word on the mining industry

It is accurate to say that mining can still generate a profit. After all, there is an ongoing need for people to work in mines. However, if you are serious about generating a constant profit through investing in cryptocurrency, the best strategy is to either learn how to trade cryptocurrencies or directly invest in a cryptocurrency. If you are serious about making a profit, you should learn how to trade cryptocurrencies. Additionally, the amount of profit that you may make by mining for cryptocurrencies is significantly lower compared to the amount of profit that you could make by investing directly in a cryptocurrency. To add insult to injury, mining a sufficient quantity of bitcoin in a day is not a task that can be accomplished without a lot of effort.

Why should we care about this? The process of chaining and confirming blocks produces new cryptocoins that are then distributed across the system. We will go into more detail about this process shortly. In addition to this, the utilization of encryption to produce a connected chain of blocks helps to ensure the reliability of the system. As was said before, it is extremely difficult, if not impossible, to reverse the process of generating a cryptographic hash within an authentic cryptocurrency system. Since the data in the blocks that came before it is timestamped and then converted into a cryptographic hash, there is no way for any data in the bitcoin network as a whole to be stolen. The entire cryptocurrency system is not safe and is vulnerable to assaults or crucial flaws if the procedure of chaining together individual blocks into a blockchain is not implemented.

On what kind of network do all of these different procedures get carried out? A distributed ledger is a type of network that underpins blockchain technology and, by extension, cryptocurrencies in general. This is a special kind of network that brings together a number of different networks into one unified and synchronized database of digital information.

A distributed ledger is the foundation upon which cryptocurrencies are constructed, and this ledger is used to facilitate the sharing of the data generated by blockchain technology. Because everyone in the network possesses a copy of the blockchain that is both identical and up to date, each user in the network holds the others accountable for their actions. Let's take a peek at the workings of a distributed ledger to see how a cryptocurrency system keeps track of transactions.

A distributed ledger is a type of digital ledger that stores and verifies data across the whole network of users. The blockchain is something that is saved on each every client in a cryptocurrency system. Users are required to provide updates to one another and verify any new modifications made to the blockchain whenever there is a change made to it. All participants on the distributed ledger are responsible for maintaining an identical and up-to-date copy of the blockchain even if there is no need for a centralized server to do so. A mathematical algorithm that is referred to as a consensus algorithm is the procedure that leads to the achievement of this consensus. In addition to cryptocurrency systems such as Bitcoin, there are a number of financial institutions that make use of distributed ledgers in order to reduce the risk of potential losses.

New cryptocoins need to be generated on a consistent basis, just like any other type of currency. The act of creating new cryptocurrencies through a process known as mine is referred to as "mining." Mining is the process of adding new records of transactions to the public ledger that is maintained by the blockchain. Mining is done to keep the distributed ledger of transaction data up to date, but there is another purpose that mining serves as well. Each time a block is successfully mined, the miner receives a reward in the form of a unit of the cryptocurrency being mined as a thank you for their contribution to the creation of the blockchain. The mining of bitcoins is comparable to the mining of gold in this regard. Mining becomes increasingly challenging as more and more Bitcoins are extracted from the ground.

The field in the blockheader that was discussed before is responsible for controlling the level of complexity of a mining operation. The word "difficult" might be used to describe this area. Mining becomes increasingly harder as more blocks are added to the network. The reward that is paid to miners gradually lowers as time goes on as well. Because of this, the total number of cryptocoins that may be mined is restricted. As is the case with physical resources, the availability of the resource decreases over time, making it increasingly harder to obtain more of it. This indicates that cryptocurrencies such as Bitcoin often have a predetermined cap placed on the total number of units of cryptocoin that may be mined. Due to the limited supply of cryptocoin units, their value has increased.

Modify the Moving Averages You Use

Which moving averages to display is already selected in most chart software. These are frequently the 9 and 18-day averages, 9 and 26-day averages, or 50 and 200-day averages, for example.

However, these may not be your ideal averages. Avoid making the mistake of relying solely on a charting website to choose the appropriate moving averages to employ.

For example, you should obtain something like 5-8-13 bar averages if you have made the decision to become a day trader. Price bars are available for every hour, every five minutes, or even every minute, so your average may be 5-8-13 minutes rather than 5-8-13 days. However, be cautious since they may provide excellent indications when the market is doing well. However, during turbulent trading, they can be all over the place, so it's better to declare a time out, go flat (selling all of your holdings), and have a coffee.

Look at longer-term averages like the 26 and 50-day SMAs or EMAs if you trade longer periods. Along with the 50-day MA, 20/21 are useful for swing traders; the slower average is well-matched with the 200 and 250-period MAs.

Keep in mind that because the EMA moves more swiftly than the SMA, it will identify trades earlier. However, this comes at a cost, as the EMA will provide you with more false signals than the SMA. The EMA will get you into a price swing faster if you're happy making lots of trades and closing the losers quickly. However, if you want to trade longer-term and hold onto your positions longer, SMAs will give you winning trades that are marginally less profitable overall but fewer stopped-out trades and fewer trades overall.

One of the reasons why MAs are successful is that almost everybody uses them. It is possible that calculating a moving average over the last 34 days will not provide you with any information that is valuable or that can be used to make decisions. You could give it a shot, backtest it on a few other charts, and see what happens. However, I highly doubt that you will really discover that it is a covert weapon. I gave a couple of them a shot, but they were never successful for me.

And last, when there is no discernible trend in the market, moving averages are completely useless. Do not attempt to utilise the MAs as a source of trading ideas while the market is in a ranging state since these ideas are going to be all over the place and will simply lead you into trouble. Wait until you can once again make out a distinct pattern.

Moving Averages (MA) The MOVING AVERAGE (MA) trading method is frequently utilised in the cryptocurrency trading industry to regularise price activity over a particular time span. It is a lagging indicator that is calculated based on the price behaviour from the past. Moving averages may be broken down into two distinct categories: the SIMPLE MOVING AVERAGE and the EXPONENTIAL MOVING AVERAGE. Traders often select their favourite MA type in accordance with the trading technique that they employ. If you trade in the short term, you should choose a moving average that is shorter since it will function better with your strategy. On the other hand, a lengthier MA is appropriate for a trader who is looking at the market for the long term. When it comes to trading, the moving average may act as either a support or a resistance.

The Positives and Negatives of Obtaining an MA

Moving averages are easy mathematical formulae that were developed to analyse and assess specific data points across a range of time periods. They do this by averaging the values of those points over time. As a consequence of this, it generates a graphical instrument that merchants may use to prompt them as to whether or not they should engage a transaction or take a position.

In addition to this, MA may be used to determine stop-loss thresholds and designate exit points. Because of this quality, the technique is one of the most useful tools that traders have at their disposal. When chart patterns are used as confirmations, MA helps traders to design a trading strategy that is more likely to be successful.

Moving averages can be calculated over any period of time; hence, it is essential to the tool's operation that the time frames be determined such that they are the most accurate or typical possible. The 50, 100, and 200 Moving Averages are the ones that are utilised the most frequently by traders.

www.ingramcontent.com/pod-product-compliance
Lightning Source LLC
Chambersburg PA
CBHW071229210326
41597CB00016B/1993